The Hydrosphere

Illustrations: Janet Moneymaker
Design/Editing: Marjie Bassler

The Hydrosphere
ISBN 978-1-953542-19-9

Published by Gravitas Publications Inc.
Imprint: Real Science-4-Kids
www.gravitaspublications.com
www.realscience4kids.com

Do you ever play in the rain?

I do when it is hot outside!

Have you ever watched water flowing in a river?

I like to swim in water.

Have you ever wondered where
the clouds and rivers get their water?

The **hydrosphere** is made up of all the water on Earth.

That is A LOT of water!

The hydrosphere includes all the water in lakes, rivers, oceans,and under the ground. It also includes rain, snow, ice, and the water in clouds.

Water exists in three forms.

1. **Liquid** (water that flows)
2. **Solid** (ice and snow)
3. **Water vapor** (gas in clouds)

Water changes from solid to liquid and from liquid to water vapor. Water also changes from water vapor to liquid to solid.

Water moves around Earth in what is called the **water cycle**.

During the water cycle, some of the water in the oceans and rivers turns into water vapor and goes into the air to form clouds. Rain and snow from the clouds return water to the oceans and rivers. These steps repeat over and over.

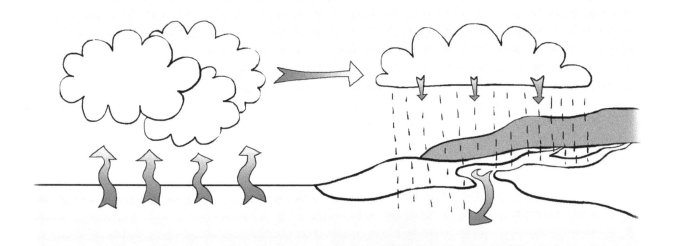

The Water Cycle

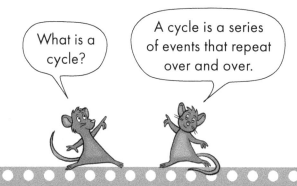

Water is very important for life on Earth. All living things need water.

Some people are not careful about keeping our water clean. Other people do things to help keep water clean.

We can help by picking up trash wherever we see it.

Yes!

Scientists are working on new ways to clean Earth's water so living things can stay healthy.

I want to learn more!

Me too!

How to say science words

hydrosphere (HIY-droh-sfeer)

liquid (LIH-kwuhd)

science (SIY-ens)

scientist (SIY-uhn-tist)

solid (SAH-luhd)

water cycle (WA-tuhr SIY-kuhl)

water vapor (WA-tuhr VAY-puhr)

What questions do you have about
THE HYDROSPHERE?

Learn More Real Science!

**Complete science curricula
from Real Science-4-Kids**

Focus On Series

Unit study for elementary and middle school levels

**Chemistry
Biology
Physics
Geology
Astronomy**

Exploring Science Series

Graded series for levels K–8. Each book contains 4 chapters of:

**Chemistry
Biology
Physics
Geology
Astronomy**

CPSIA information can be obtained
at www.ICGtesting.com
Printed in the USA
BVHW021456310322
633014BV00005B/42

9 781953 542199